SCOTLAND

The Creation of its
Natural Landscape

Scottish Natural Heritage
Dualchas Nàdair na h-Alba
All of nature for all of Scotland
Nàdar air fad airson Alba air fad

www.snh.gov.uk

Acknowledgments
Authors: Alan McKirdy and Roger Crofts (both SNH)
The authors gratefully acknowledge constructive comments made by Doug Fettes (BGS), Magnus Magnusson, John Gordon and Rob Threadgould (all SNH)
Series Editor: Alan McKirdy (SNH)
Design and production: SNH Design and Publications

Photography: BGS 7 top left, 7 bottom right, 11 centre, **Martyn Colbeck/Oxford Scientific** 17 left, **Roger Crofts/SNH** 29 top, 32 top left, 32 bottom left, 33 bottom right, **J.A. Dunlop** 19, **Ray Ellis/Oxford Scientific** 22, **Glasgow Museum: Fossil Grove** 20, **Lorne Gill/SNH** 12, 22 bottom, 28 left, 28 top right, 28 bottom right, 33 top right, 34 bottom, 40, 43 left, 54&55, 58&59, **Patricia & Angus Macdonald** front cover, 13, 16, 20 left, 25 top, 25 bottom, 27 top, 31, 32 top right, 32 bottom right, 33 top left, 33 centre left, 33 bottom left, 33 centre right, 33 bottom right, 34 top, 36, 38, 43 top, 43 bottom right, 44&45, 46&47, 48&49, 50&51, 52&53, 54 left, 56&57, 58 left, **Steve Moore** 52 left, **National Galleries of Scotland** 6, 7 bottom left, **Natural History Museum** 21, **Suzie Stevenson/Trustees of the National Museum of Scotland** 10 top, 11 left and right, 20, **Science Photo Library** 1, 17 right, **Eysteinn Tryggvason** 24 top.

Illustrations: Craig Ellery all, except:
10 **Richard Bonson**, 18 Diagram drawn after **NH Trewin**, 19 Diagram drawn after **NH Trewin**, 29 Diagram drawn after **C Ballantyne and C Harris**, 30 Diagram drawn after **CM Clapperton**, 31 Diagram drawn after **HH Birks and RW Mathewes**, 33 Diagram drawn after **KM Clayton**, 35 Diagram drawn after **C Ballantyne and C Harris**, 37 Diagram drawn after **S Pegler, S Morrison, DE Smith, RA Cullingford, RL Jones**; 38 Diagram drawn after **GS Boulton**; JD Peacock and DG Sutherland.

ISBN: 978 1 85397 671 1

Print code TCP2K1010

Further copies are available from: Publications,
Scottish Natural Heritage, Battleby, Redgorton, Perth PH1 3EW
Tel 01738 458530 Fax 01738 456613 pubs@snh.gov.uk

Front Cover:
A view of the Torridonian sandstones of Ben Mor Coigach in the foreground with Stac Pollaidh and Suilven beyond.

SCOTLAND
The Creation of its Natural Landscape

A Landscape Fashioned by Geology

by

Alan McKirdy and Roger Crofts

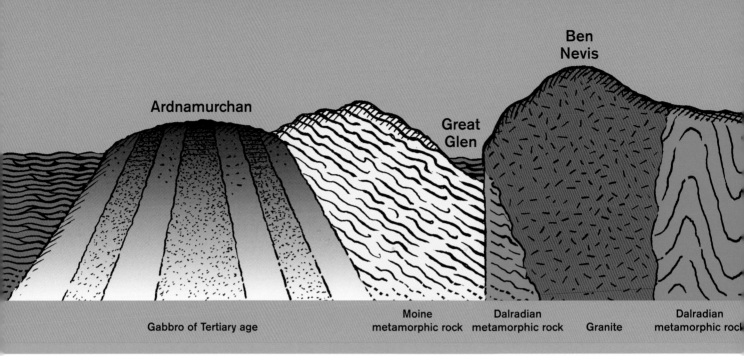

Ardnamurchan

Great Glen

Ben Nevis

Gabbro of Tertiary age

Moine metamorphic rock

Dalradian metamorphic rock

Granite

Dalradian metamorphic rock

Contents

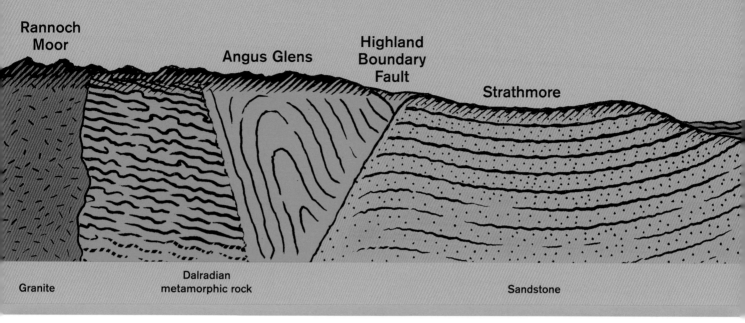

A slice of Scotland - cross section from Ardnamurchan to Montrose

Rannoch Moor

Angus Glens

Highland Boundary Fault

Strathmore

Granite

Dalradian metamorphic rock

Sandstone

Colliding continents, erupting volcanoes and moving ice sheets are some of the ways in which the diversity of Scotland's natural landscape was created. In the distant geological past, Scotland travelled towards the South Pole and wandered the southern hemisphere, before drifting to its present latitude. In the process it passed through all the Earth's climatic zones. The landmass which we now call Scotland carried an ever-changing cargo of plants and animals, many of them now extinct. For its size, Scotland has the most varied geology and natural landscape of any country on the planet. The creation of this natural landscape is a fascinating story, barely believable in part and certainly never dull.

Geological Pioneers

Scotland gave the study of geology to the world. Dr James Hutton (1726 -1797), who lived and worked in Edinburgh during the period of the Scottish Enlightenment, was the first to challenge the conventional view of the age of the Earth. Interpretation of the scriptures by Archbishop Ussher in 1658 gave a precise figure of 4,004 years BC and anyone who challenged this view was regarded as a dangerous heretic. Hutton made many geological observations during his extensive travels in Britain and across Europe.

He considered that the "vast proportion of present rocks are composed of more ancient formations"; in other words, sedimentary rocks, such as sandstones and shales, are the product of older strata which have been 'recycled'. Hutton thought that this continuous recycling process took place in long-disappeared oceans over aeons of geological time, as sediments were carried to the sea by rivers. And so it proved. In these processes, Hutton could see "no vestige of a beginning and no prospect of an end". So began his challenge to the established view of the age of the Earth. We now reliably estimate the age of the Earth as around 4,500 million years. Publication of his *Theory of the Earth* in 1788 secured for James Hutton enduring recognition as the father of modern geology and an important place in the annals of the history of science.

Raeburn's portrait of Hutton

Hugh Miller, a stonemason from Cromarty, also made a major contribution to the development of the subject. In 1841 he published a collection of articles entitled *The Old Red Sandstone* describing the wealth of fish remains fossilised in the sandstones of his local area. His popular scientific accounts were widely read.

In 1835 Britain became the first country in the world to establish a geological survey and much of the early work was undertaken in Scotland. Benjamin Peach and John Horne were foremost among the surveyors, working in the Highlands during the summer and in the Southern Uplands during the colder months. They produced geological maps, many of which have not been bettered to this day, and accompanying memoirs which provided the first detailed description of the rocks, fossils and landforms of Scotland.

Scotland also had a number of pioneers in glaciation, stimulated no doubt by the visit to Scotland of Louis Agassiz, the eminent Swiss glaciologist, in 1840. One was T. F. Jamieson, an estate factor from Ellon. He studied the deposits of the Ice Age in Scotland during the mid-nineteenth century. He was the first to recognise that the land mass was weighed down by the thickness of ice which accumulated during the Ice Age and that it rose again when the ice melted.

Osteolepis - a lobed finned fish considered to be the evolutionary ancestor of most land animals

The Assynt area of the Northwest Highlands is one of the most varied and complex geological areas in Scotland. Peach and Horne returned there many times to unravel the complexities of the rock structures and in 1907 published their classic geological memoir entitled *The Geological Structure of the Northwest Highlands of Scotland.*

The Victorian geologists, J. Horne, B. N. Peach and C. T. Clough from the Geological Survey

Geological map of Assynt

Scotland Through Time

QUATERNARY
2.4 million years ago to present day

Present day material still moving down slopes and into river systems and some of it out to sea; new river terraces being formed at lower levels; sandy coasts in some places eroding and in other places accumulating; freezing and thawing of the ground continues with further development of periglacial landforms on the mountains.
5,000 years ago, sea levels rose up to 10m higher than the present, forming beaches around the sheltered parts of the coast.
10,000 years ago, final disappearance of mountain glaciers leaving re-shaped corries, new moraines and other debris; widespread occurrence of freezing and thawing leaving extensive areas of periglacial landforms.
15,000 years ago, the last Ice Age sheet began to thaw, meltwater cut new valleys and gorges, many quickly abandoned; valleys filled with sand and gravel, and estuaries with silt and clay, Many glacial deposits, especially eskers, kame terraces and kettleholes formed.
2.4 million years to 15,000 years ago, repeated growth and decay of ice sheets and glaciers with little evidence preserved from earlier glacial periods. Formation of major features of glacial erosion, such as troughs, corries, straightening of valleys, removal of weathered bedrock and uncovering of tors.
2.4 million years ago, major cooling of the climate with onset of Ice Age.

TERTIARY
65 to 2..4 million years ago

Development of a chain of volcanoes from Skye to Ailsa Craig, as the North Atlantic formed and Scotland drifted away from Laurentia. North Sea filled as sediments were carried eastwards by rivers draining the Scottish Highlands. The climate was sub-tropical for much of the time.

CRETACEOUS
65 to 135 million years ago

For much of this period, Scotland, with the exception of the highest ground, lay under a tropical sea. Thick layers of chalk were laid down on the sea floor, but were later removed by erosion.

JURASSIC
135 to 205 million years ago

Rapid sea-level rise marked the beginning of the Jurassic period, flooding much of Scotland. Meat and plant-eating dinosaurs roamed the coastal fringes and an abundance of sea-life existed including ammonites, sea lilies (crinoids) and corals.

TRIASSIC
205 to 250 million years ago

Scotland was located in near-equatorial latitudes, in a similar position to sub-Saharan Africa today, and desert conditions largely prevailed. Red sandstones of the Elgin area, formed under these conditions preserving the footprints of long-extinct reptiles.

PERMIAN
250 to 290 million years ago

Desert conditions. Violent earthquakes rocked Scotland causing widespread folding and faulting.

CARBONIFEROUS
290 to 360 million years ago

Scotland sat astride the equator. Rainforest covered much of the Midland Valley and coral reefs flourished in the adjacent tropical seas. Numerous volcanoes erupted lava flows and ash to form the Campsie Fells, with the Arthur's Seat, North Berwick Law and Garlton Hills volcanoes also active.

DEVONIAN
360 to 410 million years ago

The high mountains created by colliding continents were rapidly eroded and the debris carried to lower ground by streams and rivers. Layer upon layer of red sandstone was deposited in freshwater lakes, some containing the remains of primitive fish and early plants.

SILURIAN
410 to 440 million years ago

The Laurentian continent collided with Avalonia as the Iapetus Ocean closed, so uniting Scotland with England and Wales. The movement took place along the major faults to assemble Scotland from four previously separate continental fragments. Many granites and related igneous rocks date back to this period.

ORDOVICIAN
440 to 510 million years ago

The Iapetus Ocean was at its widest as thick layers of sands and muds were laid down on the ocean floor. The remains of primitive life forms, such as graptolites and early corals, are preserved in these rocks. Towards the end of the Ordovician, the Iapetus Ocean narrowed considerably.

CAMBRIAN
510 to 550 million years ago

The Durness Limestones and quartzites were laid down as beach and near-shore sediments; the Pipe Rock preserves evidence of early life in the form of trumpet-shaped worm burrows.

PRECAMBRIAN
550 to 3 billion years ago

Great thicknesses of sandstone, limestone, muds and lava accumulated during later Precambrian times, which were later altered to form the rocks of the Dalradian. The earliest traces of life to be found anywhere in Scotland have been described from rocks of this age on Islay. Similarly, Moine rocks started life as layer upon layer of sandstone, only to be altered by deep burial in the Earth's crust. Torridonian sandstones accumulated at much the same time and have remained largely unaltered. However, the oldest rocks in Scotland, by far, are the Lewisian gneisses, which are interpreted as part of the Earth's crust, as it existed up to 3 billion years ago.

Geological Column

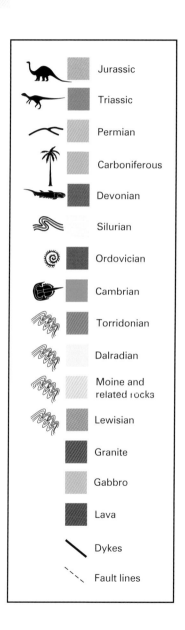

	Jurassic
	Triassic
	Permian
	Carboniferous
	Devonian
	Silurian
	Ordovician
	Cambrian
	Torridonian
	Dalradian
	Moine and related rocks
	Lewisian
	Granite
	Gabbro
	Lava
	Dykes
	Fault lines

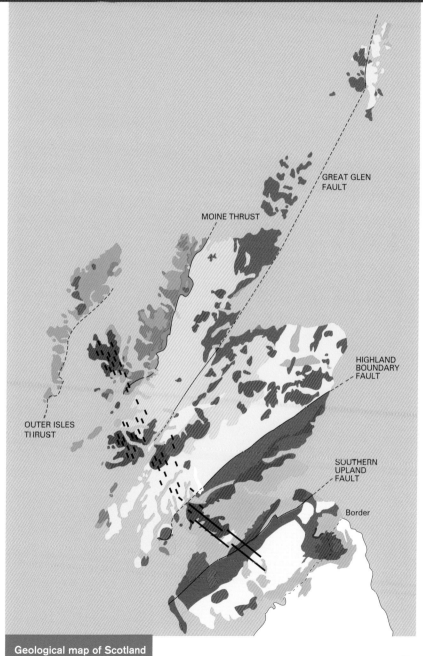

GREAT GLEN FAULT

MOINE THRUST

HIGHLAND BOUNDARY FAULT

OUTER ISLES THRUST

SOUTHERN UPLAND FAULT

Border

Geological map of Scotland

Drifting Continents

Reptile footprints in sandstone

The geological story of Scotland is recorded in its bedrock and is also the logical starting point from which to describe Scotland's natural heritage. Planet Earth formed after the Big Bang, with our present atmosphere, land and sea derived from the molten core of the primordial planet. Since these beginnings, continental land masses have moved across the globe, coming together and parting in a multitude of configurations. Rock masses, hundreds of square kilometres in size, broke away from the main continental areas and became welded to adjacent landmasses, linking areas which had no previous association. This process of continental drift created a series of patchwork landmasses, with Scotland forming a small part of a major continent which included North America and Greenland, known as Laurentia. At this time over 500 million years ago, Scotland was separated from England and Wales by an ocean wider than the present-day Atlantic. The Iapetus Ocean closed around 410 million years ago uniting Scotland and England forever! Over time, this landmass has moved through all the Earth's climatic zones, only to split asunder around 60 million years ago when the North Atlantic was formed.

This globe depicts how a map of the world may have looked 500 million years ago. Scotland (A), located south of Greenland, was a little piece of Laurentia, separated from Avalonia (England and Wales) (B) by the Iapetus Ocean.

Scotland has drifted across the surface of the planet like a great Ark, constructed of rock rather than wood, and driven not by the tides and winds, but by the movement of plates on the Earth's surface. It carried a varied cargo of plants and animals. These early forms of life had to adapt to the ever-changing environmental conditions - or die out. Evidence for deep oceans, scalding deserts and tropical rainforests are all to be found in Scotland's record of the rocks. And so, the early inhabitants evolved to fit these environmental niches.

Crinoid or sea lily which grew in warm tropical seas | Trilobite which inhabited the Iapetus Ocean | Fern which grew in a tropical rainforest

Rocks dating back 3 billion years are to be found in the Western Isles, on Coll, Tiree, Iona and the Rhinns of Islay, and along a coastal strip of the Northwest Highlands from Cape Wrath to Kyle of Lochalsh. These banded rocks, called Lewisian 'gneiss' (pronounced 'nice'), were formed many kilometres down in the crust and were gradually exposed at the surface as earth movements pushed them upwards. Over time, wind, water and ice wore away the covering rocks and this ancient crust was exposed at the surface. These are the oldest known rocks in Scotland and are among the most ancient to be found anywhere in the world.

The imposing glens around Applecross and Torridon are built of red sandstones which were dumped in vast thicknesses on top of this primordial crust of Lewisian gneiss. Large rivers flowed eastwards from higher ground, depositing layer upon layer of sand and pebbles at the edge of the continent of Laurentia which lay, at that time, south of the Equator. These Torridonian strata are largely restricted to the Northwest Highlands with smaller occurrences on Skye, Rum, Iona, Colonsay and Islay. The Durness Limestones lie on top of the Torridonian sandstones, and also form part of the ancient crust. These limestones and associated sandstones are interpreted as

The Ancient Crust

Roadcutting in Lewisian gneiss - Loch Laxford

Suilven is made from Torridonian sandstone, capped by Cambrian strata. It rests on a platform of Lewisian gneiss which has been exposed millions of years later by ice

beach deposits marking the coastal fringe of Laurentia. Beneath tranquil seas, sands, silts and limy muds were deposited, containing evidence of early life. This, the Cambrian period, is characterised by a profusion of new life-forms world-wide, some of which are preserved in the Durness Limestones.

The foundations for the Scottish Highlands were also being laid at this time. Thick sequences of sandstone, shales and limestones were deposited, later to be altered or metamorphosed by heat and pressure related to subsequent earth movements - primarily those generated when continents collided. These Dalradian (named after the ancient Scots Kingdom of Dalriada) and Moine rocks occupy much of the ground north of the Highland Boundary Fault. Despite their turbulent origins, the Dalradian rocks provide evidence for some of the earliest life-forms in Scotland, indeed in the world. Small pellet-like features found on Islay are dung pellets produced by soft-bodied creatures, such as worms, which inhabited these ancient sediments.

Evidence is also preserved in the Dalradian rocks of glacial activity, indicating that Scotland was subjected to an ice age at a time when it was located close to the South Pole!

Continents Collide

Until 410 million years ago, the area of land now recognised as Scotland was separated from England by an ocean wider than the present-day North Atlantic - the Iapetus Ocean. When the two halves of Britain, which were part of separate larger continental land masses, began to drift towards each other, so the Iapetus Ocean began to close inexorably. The seaway between the converging continents narrowed until they collided and mountains were squeezed up in place of the vanished ocean. The two ancient continents, originally on opposite sides of the vast ocean, were now joined along a line known as the Iapetus Suture which runs almost parallel to Hadrian's Wall.

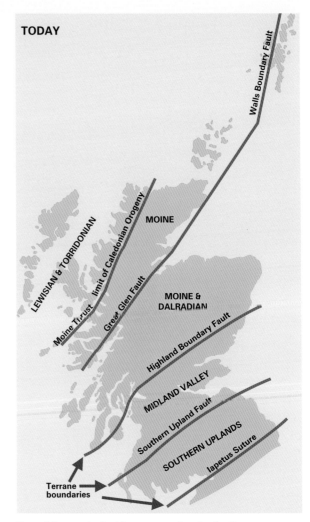

Map of the geological terranes and major faults

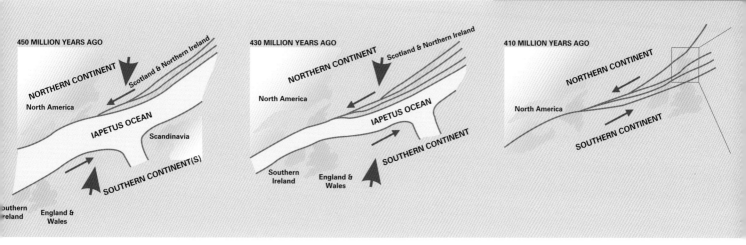

450 MILLION YEARS AGO

NORTHERN CONTINENT
North America
Scotland & Northern Ireland
IAPETUS OCEAN
Scandinavia
SOUTHERN CONTINENT(S)
Southern Ireland
England & Wales

430 MILLION YEARS AGO

NORTHERN CONTINENT
North America
Scotland & Northern Ireland
IAPETUS OCEAN
SOUTHERN CONTINENT
Southern Ireland
England & Wales

410 MILLION YEARS AGO

NORTHERN CONTINENT
North America
SOUTHERN CONTINENT

Scotland's geological diversity is largely derived from this continental collision. Prior to closure, the land which was to become Scotland was, in fact, a series of distinct geological 'terranes' separated by major geological faults.

As the Iapetus Ocean closed, so the disparate terranes slid together side by side to form one contiguous landmass and then joined with England. In geological terms, the 'union' of Scotland with England took place around 410 million years ago.

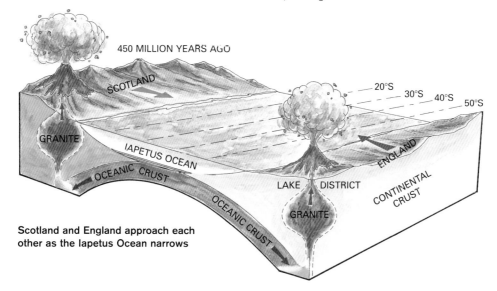

450 MILLION YEARS AGO

SCOTLAND
GRANITE
IAPETUS OCEAN
OCEANIC CRUST
OCEANIC CRUST
LAKE DISTRICT
GRANITE
ENGLAND
CONTINENTAL CRUST
20°S
30°S
40°S
50°S

Scotland and England approach each other as the Iapetus Ocean narrows

15

Colliding continents have given rise to some of Scotland's most familiar scenic views and landmarks. The Highland Boundary Fault, a terrane boundary, cuts across the south end of Loch Lomond. This Highland - Lowland boundary shown on the photograph reflects the major geological change from hard Dalradian metamorphic rock in the background to the pebbley conglomorates and softer sandstones of Devonian age in the foreground.

The line of the fault is marked by an intrusion of serpentine, forming much of Conic Hill and Inchcailloch Island. This very base-rich material was derived from great depths in the Earth's crust. The 'Highland Line' marks a sharp change in topography, weather, vegetation, wildlife and landuse. It also played an important part in Scotland's historical and cultural development.

INCHCAILLOCH   CONIC HILL

Conic Hill, Inchcailloch and the south end of Loch Lomond mark the line of the Highland Boundary Fault, an important 'terrane boundary'

Mount Everest, in the Mount Everest or Sagamatha National Park, illustrates the probable scale of the Dalradian mountains

rocks of Dalradian and Moine, comprising mainly schists and quartzites (the latter having the strength of steel), are also resistant to erosion, so have remained as relatively high ground since they were formed. And so the Scottish Highlands were born.

The relationship between geology and landscape is clearly reflected in the Landsat image below. The harder more resistant crystalline rocks of the Highlands form the higher ground, separated from the Midland Valley by the Highland Boundary Fault. Many of the other major displacements, such as the Great Glen Fault and Southern Upland Fault, are also clearly visible.

A mountain range perhaps as high as the Himalayas was created as a result of the Scotland - England collision. Great masses of granite and related rocks were formed from molten magma injected deep into the Earth's crust. However, as the great peaks that must have existed then were worn down by ice and water over many millions of years, these granites and their darker, more base-rich equivalent rocks, known as gabbros, were exposed at the Earth's surface. The Cairngorms, Ben Nevis and many other significant hills and mountains throughout Scotland are carved from granite formed at this time. The altered

A satellite view of Scotland which shows a clear link between geology and landscape

Devonian Lakes and Hot Springs

Reconstruction of what Lake Orcadie would have looked like during Devonian times

The mountains surrounding the lake, which has now come to be called Lake Orcadie, were eroding rapidly as rivers cut through the barren high ground. Enormous volumes of mud and sand were transported along these river systems to the shores of the lake which teemed with primitive life-forms of the most bizarre construction. Armour-plated fish, now long extinct, and the precursors of the species we see on the fishmonger's slab today, were found in profusion in Lake Orcadie. Evidence for great shoals of these monsters is provided in particular rock horizons, called 'fish beds'. These special layers are finely banded, indicating a very slow rate of sediment accumulation in the deepest part of the lake, with each layer representing the sediment input for one year. Like counting the rings of a tree stump, the length of time represented by a particular fish bed can be readily established.

Some of the earliest insects and most primitive plants to grow on land are also preserved in rocks of a similar age to the lake sediments of Lake Orcadie. A unique deposit of chert, found near the village of Rhynie, Aberdeenshire, preserves the fossilised remains of some of the earliest land plants recorded from anywhere in the world. The deposit is an excellent example of the preservation of life-forms in an instant of geological time. An ancient marsh plant community grew close to a number of hot springs, which overflowed from time to time, flooding the adjacent wetland with silica-rich boiling water.

After the storm of colliding continents came a period of calm. At this time in geological history, the evolving Britain sat some 10° south of the equator, and Laurentia was joined, as one landmass, to North America and Greenland. Much of Scotland was made up of high mountainous areas of alpine proportions, with a few isolated freshwater basins fringing this super-continent. It was in one of these large lakes and its associated rivers and deltas that the Orkney Islands were born.

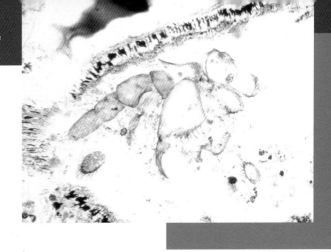

This deadly cocktail cooled quickly, trapping plants and insects in a Pompeii-like act of instantaneous preservation. This primitive time capsule has been much studied by scientists around the world and, as a result, a great deal has been learned about the early life-forms which inhabited planet Earth 400 million years ago. The Rhynie Chert locality was recently gifted to Scottish Natural Heritage ensuring that this world-renowned place will be preserved for many future generations of geologists to study.

How the hot springs and plant communities at Rhynie may have looked

Coal Swamps and Volcanoes

With time, the freshwater lakes which characterised the Devonian period disappeared and the age of the coal swamp began - the Carboniferous. At this time, Scotland was located on the equator, so the widespread tropical vegetation which clothed the landscape flourished in response to the hot and humid conditions. The early part of this geological period was marked by vast outpourings of lava that spewed out across the Midland Valley to build, for example, the Campsie Fells and Gargunnock Hills.

Fossil tree stumps at Fossil Grove, Victoria Park, Glasgow

The Gargunnock Hills showing the sequence of lava which accumulated layer upon layer

The step-like profile of these hills reflects their structure, built as they are of layer upon layer of lava. Around volcanoes in the Midland Valley, tropical swamps developed made up of many species of trees and ferns, most of which are long extinct. As the individual trees of these ancient tropical forests died, they fell into the swamp, eventually to form layers rich in organic carbon. As more sediment accumulated on top, these carbon-rich layers were compressed to form coal. Vast riches of fossil fuel accumulated during this period, which were, some 350 million years later, to bankroll the Industrial Revolution in

Scotland. Exploitation of these resources continues today and geologists have built up a detailed knowledge of the nature and distribution of these deposits.

The first action to conserve Scotland's geological heritage was initiated in 1887 when a number of fossil tree stumps were unearthed in what is now Victoria Park in Glasgow. In recognition of the great scientific and cultural significance of these tree stumps, a building was erected to protect them from fossil collectors and the ravages of the elements. This building was recently renovated by Glasgow City Council.

Another jewel from the Carboniferous period was found in Bathgate, near Edinburgh. It was here that a rare fossil called 'Lizzie' or *Westlothiana lizziae* was found. Lizzie is the fossilised remains of the oldest reptile to be found anywhere in the world and its discovery has been described as one of the finds of the century. It was previously thought that reptiles evolved later in the Carboniferous period, so this chance find has overturned evolutionary theory of the early development of this important animal group.

During the Permian, parts of Scotland would have resembled this Namibian desert scene

Deserts and Dinosaurs

Terraced houses in Perth made from red sandstone illustrate how these rocks have been used

During the next 70 million years, the tropical swamps disappeared to be replaced by deserts as 'Scotland' continued its slow northward wandering. High ground still occupied much of the country. Only isolated areas of red sandstone survive to record the climatic conditions which existed during Permian and Triassic times. Scotland remained in near-equatorial latitudes, in a similar position to sub-Saharan Africa today and, in the main, desert conditions prevailed. Many of the fine red sandstone buildings that exist in Scotland owe their origin to these 260 million-year-old desert sands preserved in the Mauchline and Dumfries areas, from where they have been quarried extensively during the last two centuries.

Desert conditions also gripped the Moray area during Triassic times. The remains of small reptiles and their fossilised trackways have been recovered from the sandstones around Elgin - some from a working quarry where prompt action was required to save them from the crusher!

For reasons not fully understood, but probably related to a catastrophic meteor strike on Earth around 65 million years ago, the dinosaur dynasty died out, never to return in Scotland or, indeed, anywhere else on the planet.

Reconstruction of the flesh-eating Skye dinosaur, *Ceratosaur*

Then came a flood of biblical proportions as the sea level rose to inundate much of Scotland. This dramatic event marked the beginning of the Jurassic period. Erosion has removed all but a few remnants of the carpet of marine sands and muds which were laid down under these rising seas. Over time, sea levels fell and the emergent land was rapidly recolonised. Among the new occupants of Skye were flesh- and plant-eating dinosaurs, now preserved in the Jurassic sediments found along the east coast of the Trotternish Peninsula. *Cetiosaurus*, a plant-eating dinosaur, stood 10m in height and is thought to be a member of the Sauropod family.

Reconstruction of a plant-eating Skye dinosaur, *Cetiosaurus*

The Atlantic Ocean Opens

'Chain of Fire' volcanic eruption, Iceland. New molten material is added to the crust, pushing continents apart

When the seas subsided, Scotland emerged to face yet another ordeal, this time by fire. Scotland was still bound to the eastern flank of North America around 65 million years ago, but yet another substantial re-arrangement of the continents created the North Atlantic Ocean. It developed as a tear in the Earth's crust, with volcanic eruptions adding new rocks along the central spine of the nascent ocean.

Scotland and North America drift progressively further apart

The associated stretching and thinning of the Earth's crust near the margin of the emergent ocean allowed molten rock to break through the crust to form a line of volcanoes running from St Kilda to Ailsa Craig. Many individual volcanoes were active over a period of about 5 million years (Ben More on Mull, Ardnamurchan, Rum, Skye, St Kilda and Rockall), throwing ash clouds high into the air and spewing out vast thicknesses of lava.

The island of Skye is perhaps the finest example of an ancient volcano whose bowels and inner plumbing have been laid bare by the elements. The scarp face and gently sloping topography of the Trotternish Peninsula and northwest Skye were fashioned from the lava fields which developed around the volcano. The boiling magma chamber, which contained molten rock by the cubic kilometre, lay underneath the lava field. It later solidified to form a rock known as gabbro. This is the Black Cuillin. The Red Cuillin was formed as the molten mass of gabbro came into contact with the lower crust causing it to melt and form a red granite. Erosion by wind, water and ice removed more than 2km of the volcano's super-structure and, as a result, the relationship between its various component parts can be studied. Indeed, the Skye volcano has been the subject of detailed geological investigations for the best part of a century and a half, and many of the ideas developed have been used to unravel the complexities of similar features around the world.

View of the Ardnamurchan volcano, showing the circular form of the magma intrusions, called ring dykes

View of Skye: the Black Cuillin on the right and the Red Cuillin on the left with the lava field in the foreground

Filling the North Sea

Crucial to the understanding of the present landscape of Scotland is the 60-million-year Tertiary period. With the fall in sea levels and the instability of the land associated with the opening of the Atlantic Ocean came a long period of humid climate. Temperatures varied but were predominantly warmer than those of today. Under these conditions, two formative activities in the evolution of the landscape can be identified: the development of river basins and the weathering of rocks.

Dramatic events were not restricted to the western seaboard. The simple answer to the question "where did all the sediment go which had covered Scotland?" is that it was deposited in the North Sea; an accumulation of up to 3,000m thickness. And why to the North Sea? For two reasons. First, the watershed between the water flowing into the Atlantic and that flowing into the North Sea was well to the west of the country and much of the land drained eastwards; second, tensions in the Earth's crust between Britain and Norway resulted in the formation of a great gash on the floor of the North Sea. It had tremendous capacity because the basin continued to deepen as the forces of the Earth tore it apart. This trench acted as the great sink for the rocks eroded from the surrounding land.

The present day landscape of the eastern Grampians around Glen Clova still exhibits the rolling scenery and step-like forms of the pre-glacial landscape

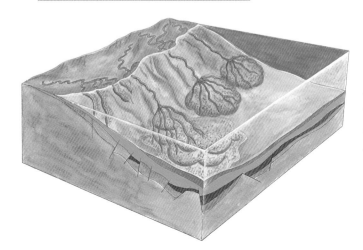

Reconstruction of the North Sea off the coast of Scotland showing the deposition of debris from adjacent land on top of the older fractured rocks

As there are virtually no rocks left on land from this period, we must rely on examination of the material deposited in the North Sea. We can date the deposits but we do not really know how fast the landscape developed. The most plausible view, now of many decades standing, is that major river systems formed on the gently tilted sediments in a classic tree-shaped pattern flowing eastwards. Many of these remain in the present landscape; for example, the Tay, Don and Dee. Gently rolling upland plains were formed, the rivers cut into the ancient rocks and carried their debris into the North Sea.

Rocks Disintegrate

Deeply weathered granite: resistant 'core stones' and less resistant gravelly material 'grus' decomposed from granite in the humid climates of the Tertiary period were only exposed after the ice caps had disappeared

conditions towards the end of the Tertiary period, chemical disintegration became less significant and physical disintegration of rocks increased to create gravelly material known as 'grus'. Weathered material often stayed in place.

Exposure of a clay material, Macaulayite, at Pittodrie, Aberdeenshire, formed in the warm, humid climates of the Tertiary period

Soil formations reminiscent of sub-tropical Africa, known as laterites, found below and baked hard by the lavas of Skye

In many parts of the Highlands, rocks of different types began to disintegrate at different speeds under the humid climatic conditions. In the early part of the Tertiary period, Scotland experienced warm humid climates similar to the sub-tropics of today, resulting in chemical disintegration of the rocks. Kaolin, a clay material, was formed. Deposits of this type are found at Pittodrie, Aberdeenshire, for instance. With the gradual cooling of the climate to more temperate

The exposed core stones of the granite tors of Beinn a'Bhuird in the Cairngorms have survived cover by the ice caps

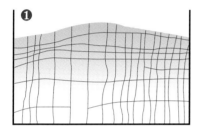 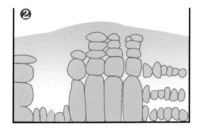 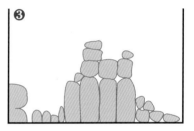

Three stages in the development of tors: ❶ jointing in the bedrock and percolation of acidic rainwater; ❷ more resistant rocks survive when surrounding rocks disintegrate chemically; ❸ removal of disintegrated rocks leaving tors at the surface

Indeed, in parts of Aberdeenshire and Buchan, for example, faces of apparently solid granite rock crumble to the touch; a handful of gravel rather than a solid piece of rock.

Smooth erosion surfaces of relatively uniform altitude are found all around the drainage basins of eastern Scotland. Below these, river valleys often open out into wider basins and it is there that the chemically weathered and physically altered rocks are to be found.

More singular and dramatic features in the landscape, especially in the granites of the Cairngorms and Aberdeenshire, are the 'tors'. These represent remnants of harder, more resistant rocks, standing sentinel-like on the high mountains. The weaker rocks which had surrounded them disintegrated and were removed by ice and solifluction, leaving the tors upstanding at the surface.

The classic theory of tor formation involves a number of steps. We start with a level or gently sloping surface of crystalline granite rocks which have vertical and horizontal cracks as a result of their shrinking on cooling and the unloading that followed the removal of the overlying rocks. Rainwater of a warm, mildly acidic type during the early Tertiary period penetrated these cracks gradually exploiting the weaknesses. Through time, core stones of the stronger and more resistant rocks were left surrounded by weathered rock debris. Later, during the period of the ice ages, the loose debris was finally removed to reveal the tors as we see them today.

The 'Ice Age'

The Ice Periods

During the 2.4 million year period commonly called the 'Ice Age', Scotland experienced a succession of cooler and warmer periods (glacials/stadials and interglacials). With these came the accumulation of ice in the form of ice caps and glaciers. Their movement, and that of the meltwater rivers associated with them, has had a significant role in fashioning the detail of the landscape we see today. Overall, however, the basic elements of the highlands and lowlands have remained as in pre-glacial times, particularly in the south and east.

Three stages of glaciation in Scotland and Europe:
1. 29-22,000 years ago with Scandinavian and Scottish ice sheets joini
2. 15-14,000 years ago with an ice cap covering most of Scotland
3. The Loch Lomond Stadial around 10,500 years ago

The climatic changes were often abrupt, measurable in decades. The weight of ice caused much of the country to be lowered; at the same time the capture of water in the ice meant that sea levels were lower. When the ice melted, vast quantities of water were released, depositing sands and gravels in river valleys and offshore. The melting also caused the sea level to rise and beaches were formed above the present sea level (now called 'raised beaches').

It is fair to assume that all of Scotland has been covered by ice at some stage during the last 2.4 million years. The ice caps and glaciers of the earlier cold periods, were undoubtedly most influential in eroding and reshaping the landscape. During the latest cold episode, from 115,000 to 10,000 years ago, there were probably several glacial stages. At the time of the last ice sheet, some hills in the West and Northwest Highlands could have stood out as 'nunataks' above the ice. The last cold period, termed the 'Loch Lomond Stadial' (the landforms were first described at the south end of Loch Lomond), occurred 11-10,000 years ago, and left moraines and outwash terraces in many valleys and small moraines in many corries.

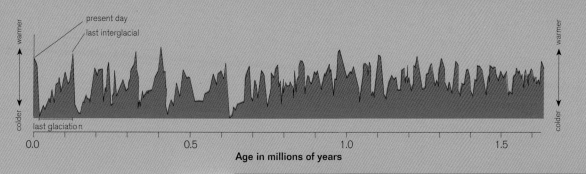

Changes in global climate during the last 1.6 million years as detected from sediments on the floor of the mid-Atlantic Ocean

We know a great deal about the effects of ice on the landscape but little of the timescales, except for the most recent events during the last 30,000 years or so as illustrated in the three maps. Ice has fashioned the landscape through erosion, smoothing and moulding the bedrock, and transporting and depositing rock debris.

Ice eroded

Ice smoothed bare rock; it removed weathered debris and helped expose the resistant tors; it created hollows or corries (some 500 of them in Scotland); it overrode the land between river catchments, breaching the watersheds (aiding later changes in the courses of rivers); it deepened valleys to form rock basins now occupied by freshwater lochs or more particularly the sea lochs of the west coast (more than 100 of them); it also smoothed rocks on the upstream side and plucked rocks on the downstream side to form 'roches moutonnées' and smoothed others to form streamlined rock outcrops such as 'crag and tail' forms. By far the greatest impact was in the West and Northwest Highlands, illustrated by the fact that 90% of the corries and more than 90% of the rock basins are in westerly flowing river systems. There rain and snowfall were greater, the ice thicker and the glaciers steeper and faster flowing.

Ice eroded: the corries and troughs of Braeriach in the Cairngorms are classic ice erosion features

Ice is thought to have had a relatively benign effect on the landscape in some areas, especially in Northeast Scotland. Many of the features of the pre-ice period, especially gently rolling surfaces and weathered bedrock, remain little modified, tors have been uncovered but not destroyed and river systems remain largely intact.

31

Glacier carrying debris, Solheimajökull, Iceland

Meltwater cut valley near West Linton

Ice carried debris

Ice is not a uniform solid and has many cracks (which means that parts of it move at different rates). Rocks and rock debris of all shapes and sizes (including tiny pieces known as 'rock flour') are frozen onto the surface, within its layers and at its base. It can carry rocks long distances before depositing them and from these 'erratics' we can tell from which direction the ice moved and how far it travelled.

Meltwater cut valleys

When ice melted it created very powerful meltwater rivers. These often followed the existing river systems, but high-water pressure can make rivers in and under the ice flow uphill, and across cols and spurs between river systems. Many of these meltwater valleys are now left dry or have streams much smaller than the valleys in which they flow. At times the meltwater spilled into valleys dammed by the ice and formed lakes whose shorelines in places like Glen Roy and Glen Gloy are still evident as the well-known 'Parallel Roads'. The lakes drained periodically under the ice in great floods.

'Hummocky moraines' of the Valley of a Hundred Hills in Torridon

Ice deposited material

Ice deposited material on the ground beneath it, when its speed was reduced and where valleys widened. Where it reached the limits of its extension it deposited 'moraines'. In places, 'hummocky' moraine in the form of hundreds of hillocks was deposited on valley floors. On lower ground, where it had less momentum, it deposited sheets of material traditionally called 'boulder clay' as it often comprises stones and boulders in a fine-grained matrix (more technically called 'till'). These deposits are perhaps the most significant of all because they are so widespread in the lowlands and upland valleys and provide the 'parent' material for many of our modern soils.

Esker at Bedshill in the Lothians

Meltwater deposited debris

It is the deposits from these meltwater streams which are most apparent in the landscape. At the side of the ice, 'kame' terraces were deposited; under the ice (usually in tunnels), sinuous ridges or 'eskers' were formed (e.g. at Carstairs) and beyond the ice margin the debris was laid down in the form of 'outwash' plains or lake deltas (e.g. at Achnasheen). The vast extent of these features in the glens and fringing the mountain masses in the east and south of Scotland, emphasises the contrast between the landscape created by the glacial erosion in the west and by deposition in the east.

Landscapes of the 'Ice Ages'

Complete domination by ice erosion with extensive knock and lochan topography in lowland and ice moulding extending to high summits

Pre-glacial landforms no longer recognisable; valleys changed to troughs with isolated mountains

Little or no erosion; weathered bedrock, frost debris and solifluction deposits on slopes. Boulder fields and tors on ridges

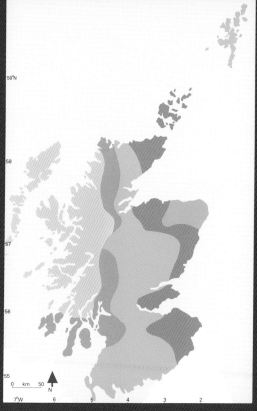

Landscape modification by Ice erosion in Scotland

Extensive excavation along ice flow lines in lowlands with isolated obstacles shaped in crag and tail forms, ice scouring of lower hills, but still some areas without erosion

Minor effects of ice erosion; some ice moulding and occasional roches moutonnées

Beyond the Ice

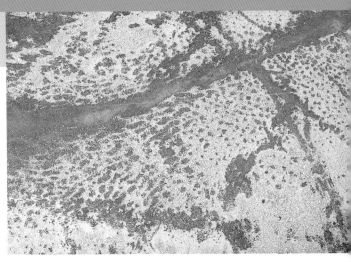

Aerial view of a blockfield with boulder sheets, lobes and sorted circles characteristic of the cold climate period on Sròn an-t saighdeir in the Western Hills of Rum

With the fluctuations in temperature during the Ice Age came fluctuations in the extent of the ice cover. The landforms created beyond the ice are a legacy of the cold climates, as are changes in the position of the coast.

With the accumulation of so much debris on the plateaux and hill slopes, and the constant freezing and thawing of the water within it, many fascinating landforms were created and can still be seen. These forms derive from what is technically termed 'periglacial' activity beyond the ice margins and can be seen being formed in arctic and alpine areas today. The freezing and thawing of the upper

These surface ripples, solifluction terraces, reflect the gradual movement down the slope of debris

levels of the ground, above permanently frozen ground below or the thawing out of an active surface layer were the formative influences.

'Blockfields' comprising large blocks of stone characterise many mountain tops and plateaux in Scotland. The finest material has been washed below the surface or has been washed or blown away altogether. The individual boulders are often rounded and associated outcrops are very regular with both horizontal and vertical joints.

Many features show how the material has moved downslope, either in an organised and well-sorted manner, or in more chaotic form, according to a combination of the speed of movement, the gradient and the type of material. Individual boulders or groups of them roll down the slope and come to rest, often ploughing into the soil and creating a wrinkle in the surface. Some are arranged into

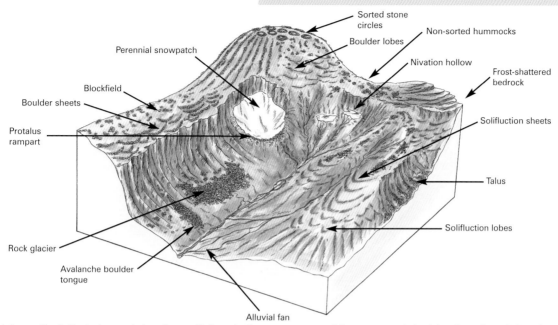

lobes with distinct step and riser forms. Soil and other coarser debris move downslope, often in the form of lobes where the material has moved to the point of some resistance and a riser has formed as a bank of turf or boulders: looking like wrinkles on jam which is about to set. More spectacular, but less frequent, is the sorting of stones into distinctive stripes downslope, with finer material in between. More widespread are debris or talus slopes, either in a uniform sheet or in cones or tongues originating from gullies and chutes. There are also areas where the entire slopes have collapsed suddenly, best seen in the Quirang of Skye and at Gribun on Mull.

Characteristic of many mountain plateaux is hummocky ground, where seasonal freezing and thawing has caused the soil surface to bulge in a regular formation. Also, there is evidence on these plateaux of the wind having blown sand and gravel, just as it does in coastal sand dunes.

Often on mountain sides there is a distinct lower limit to the forms just described; this 'trimline' marks the upper level of erosion associated with the advance of ice down a valley, trimming off the periglacial forms which were still active above the level of the ice.

On lower ground, examples of periglacial features are more difficult to see. In the gravel terraces of the river valleys, ice-wedge casts can be found where the permanently frozen ground shrank and cracked. The cracks were filled with material from the surrounding area. At a few sites, 'involutions' represent the rumpling up into folds of the soil layers through repeated freezing and thawing.

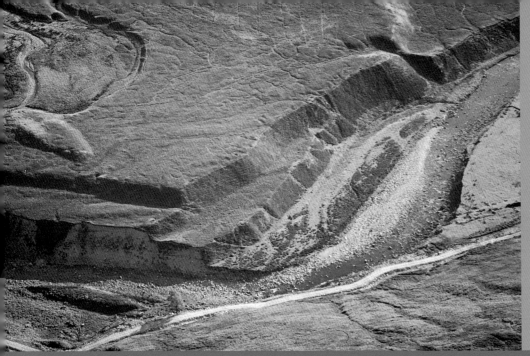

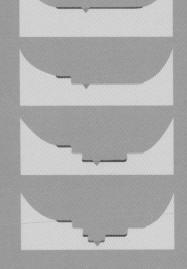

Part of the suite of terraces cut by the river in Glen Roy

Stages in the excavation of glacial valley infill by a river which has resulted in step-like terraces being formed on the valley side: the highest being the oldest

After the Ice

Whether the glacial period has ended is a moot point; hence, technically, the present period is called the 'Holocene Interglacial'. Over the last 10,000 years, since the disappearance of the ice, Scotland has experienced some variation in its climate, which has affected the landforms. But these changes are much smaller than those which occurred during the Ice Age.

Throughout the period after the ice had melted, the debris left by the ice and the meltwater has been reworked. In the river valleys, sequences of terraces have been formed as the rivers adjusted to fluctuating, but generally lower discharges. Abandoned channels are often clearly visible on them and large alluvial fans have been deposited from side valleys onto the terrace edges.

Some rivers have, naturally, continued to flood the surrounding land. Also material on slopes has continued to move downslope. Sometimes it moves in a rapid fashion especially after heavy rain in the form of landslides or debris flows. At other times movement is slower and piles against the upslope sides of drystane dykes.

Land covered by ice had no traces of soil and vegetation but we know from examination of pollen records that vegetation began to spread over the surface again from about 13,500 years ago. The speed of plant colonisation and soil development was affected by the fluctuations in climate, being held back during cold spells such as those which occurred 11-10,000 years ago, and by the acidity of surface material. Crowberry, birch and willow were early colonisers, often succeeded by ash and hazel and later by oak, elm and pine. With the advent of wetter periods, perhaps aided by the early tree felling activities of humans, came the development of peat, in many parts of the Highlands (especially the blanket bogs of Caithness and Sutherland), as well as the extensive lowland raised bogs in Central Scotland. At the same time, extensive heathlands were developing.

The development of soil and the colonisation of vegetation meant that the land surface became much more stable, and limited the amount of debris carried down the river valleys to the coast and into the sea.

The development of vegetation, as detected from pollen analysis, at two contrasting sites in Scotland over the last 10,000 years: Black Loch in Fife and Loch of Winless in Caithness. At Black Loch, woodland developed at an early stage but began to decline at the same time as the appearance of grasses and cereals, presumably reflecting early agricultural activity beginning around 5000 years ago. At Loch of Winless, open heathland with wet and dry areas existed throughout the period but overall trees declined and heathland species became more prominent.

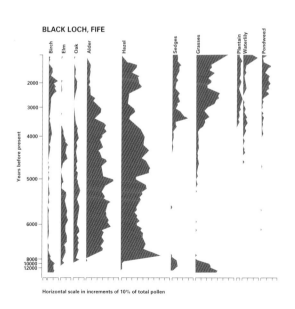

BLACK LOCH, FIFE

Horizontal scale in increments of 10% of total pollen

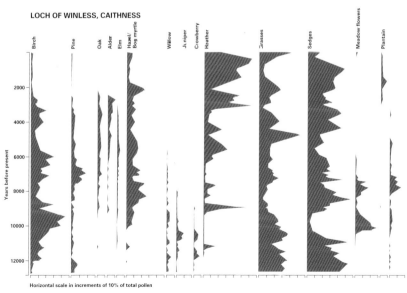

LOCH OF WINLESS, CAITHNESS

Horizontal scale in increments of 10% of total pollen

One of the most dramatic changes after the ice was the changing position of relative sea level. It has varied around Scotland, probably rising all the time in Orkney, Shetland and the Western Isles over the last 10,000 years, but elsewhere falling, then rising and then falling again. With the melting of the last ice cap, the areas depressed under its weight began to rise. The greatest uplift centred on Rannoch Moor, whereas other areas at the geographical extremities of Britain, for example, Shetland and the southeast of England, rose less or sank. At the same time, the sea level rose because of the melting of the ice globally. The variation in ice thickness in different parts of Scotland means that the amount of uplift of the land varied considerably. Hence, remnants of the higher sea levels are found at different altitudes in different parts of the country; for example, 14m in the Inner Clyde compared with 6m in the Moray Firth.

The sea level rise after the Ice Age reached its maximum around 6-7,000 years ago. The level then stayed relatively stable for up to 1,000 years before it fell gradually to its present level as the land continued to rise.

Raised beaches, with their descending shingle ridges are clear evidence of higher sea levels as can be seen here on the west coast of Jura

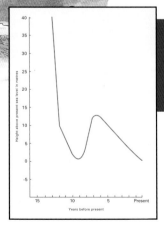

Relative sea level change in Central Scotland 15,000 years ago to the present. Note the pronounced rise 8-6,000 years ago followed by the fall to the present level

Central Scotland as it would have looked when the sea level was higher around 6 - 7,000 years ago

Layers of sediment which accumulated in caves near Assynt during the Ice Age have preserved important clues about these environments. The bones of animals no longer found in Britain, including the brown bear, reindeer, lynx and wolf, have been found. Careful detective work on these cave deposits and on pollen records from nearby sites has allowed an accurate reconstruction to be made of this area of the Northwest Highlands from the end of the Ice Age to the present day.

Much of Scotland's coast is composed of relatively resistant rocks. There are significant lengths of softer material, predominantly of sands with finer silt and muds, in shallow sheltered bays and in estuaries.

Rocky Coasts

The rocky coastlines are characterised by cliffs ranging from a few metres to a few hundred metres in height. Some end at, or near, the present sea level, whereas others plunge well below it. Some have remnants of older sea levels in the form of terraces cut into the rock, regardless of its structure or resistance, but their dates are unknown.

The Coast

The steep plunging cliffs of Esha Ness, mainland Shetland, pounded by the high energy Atlantic Ocean

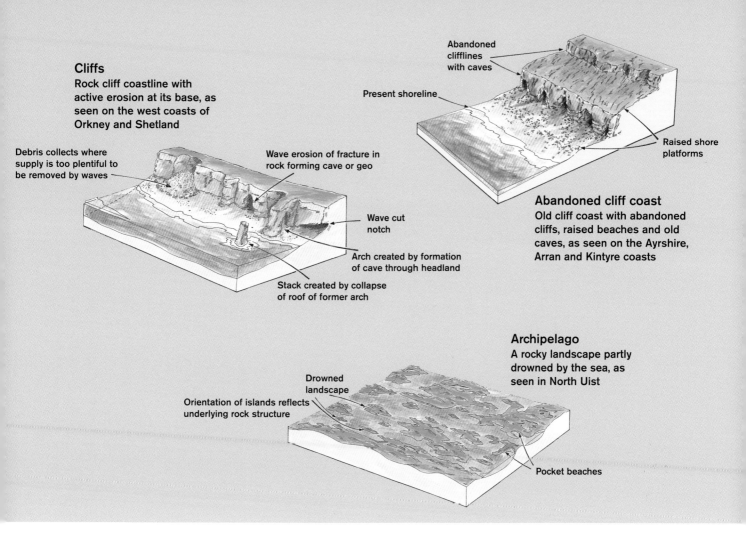

Cliffs
Rock cliff coastline with active erosion at its base, as seen on the west coasts of Orkney and Shetland

Debris collects where supply is too plentiful to be removed by waves

Wave erosion of fracture in rock forming cave or geo

Wave cut notch

Arch created by formation of cave through headland

Stack created by collapse of roof of former arch

Abandoned clifflines with caves

Present shoreline

Raised shore platforms

Abandoned cliff coast
Old cliff coast with abandoned cliffs, raised beaches and old caves, as seen on the Ayrshire, Arran and Kintyre coasts

Archipelago
A rocky landscape partly drowned by the sea, as seen in North Uist

Drowned landscape

Orientation of islands reflects underlying rock structure

Pocket beaches

Caves, headlands and bays occur alongside blow holes where part of the cave roof has collapsed, or geos where the whole roof has collapsed and from which arches and, ultimately, stacks are formed. Here the sea has exploited weaknesses in the bedding planes, joints, cracks and faults of the rocks. The processes of formation and decay of these features are still active and the powerful erosive energy of the sea is evident from the collapse of cliffs and the smoothing of the debris produced. Overall, the coast in rocky areas is perhaps best described as the accidental coincidence of the sea resting at the land edge.

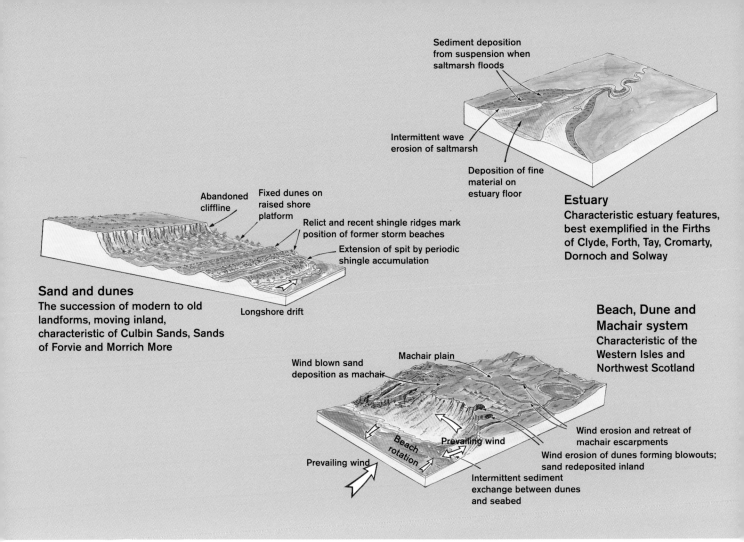

Estuary
Characteristic estuary features, best exemplified in the Firths of Clyde, Forth, Tay, Cromarty, Dornoch and Solway

Sediment deposition from suspension when saltmarsh floods

Intermittent wave erosion of saltmarsh

Deposition of fine material on estuary floor

Abandoned cliffline

Fixed dunes on raised shore platform

Relict and recent shingle ridges mark position of former storm beaches

Extension of spit by periodic shingle accumulation

Sand and dunes
The succession of modern to old landforms, moving inland, characteristic of Culbin Sands, Sands of Forvie and Morrich More

Longshore drift

Beach, Dune and Machair system
Characteristic of the Western Isles and Northwest Scotland

Machair plain

Wind blown sand deposition as machair

Prevailing wind

Beach rotation

Prevailing wind

Wind erosion and retreat of machair escarpments

Wind erosion of dunes forming blowouts; sand redeposited inland

Intermittent sediment exchange between dunes and seabed

Soft Coasts

The softer coasts are easier to date and show change more obviously. It is likely that the debris derived from glacial erosion was deposited by ice and meltwater in the present coastal area in vast amounts. What we see now is the result of a progressive redistribution over the past 14,000 years. The consequence on the coastal landscape is a series of terraces of abandoned shorelines, most prominent around the east coast firths and the Clyde. In addition, the rise of sea level enabled the coarser sands,

gravels and pebbles to be carried inland to form the basis of the large forelands of the east coast, especially Buddon Ness and Culbin, and large bars such as Montrose. With the sea level fall, a progressively lower series of shingle and sand ridges was formed by the waves at the top of the beach and then abandoned; sand was blown over the ridges and sand dune systems began to form, aided by obstructions and periodic wetting by rain, especially prominent at Culbin, Forvie and Morrich More.

At present, many of the soft coasts are being eroded, perhaps as a result of increased storminess and lack of new materials being provided by the sea.

In the West Highlands and Islands a special type of sand system, 'the machair', has evolved. It is formed almost entirely of shell fragments derived from animals living in the deeper water offshore and swept shorewards by wave action which fragmented the shells. It lacks the traditional sand dune sequence - either it was never there or it has been blown away. These sand plains owe much to human agricultural activity for their continuance.

The successive positions of shingle spits at the Culbin Sands on the Moray Firth show the gradual extension of the coast in a westerly direction towards the bottom of the picture

Characteristic machair sand plain rich with flowering plants

On many exposed coastlines, the extreme winds blow sand inland which smothers the land and forms a broad, flat plain of machair between the beaches and the hills

Landscape Cameos

By way of a series of eight landscape cameos, the relationship between geology and landscape is explored. The profound influence of rocks and landforms on the development of soils, habitats and land use is readily apparent. The most obvious distinction is between Highland and Lowland Scotland. The generally acidic rocks of the Highlands, for example, support only poor soils, so only rough grazing and traditional Highland sporting pursuits are possible there. However, this mountainous landscape provides a major economic asset, especially for the tourism industry. The Midland Valley, by contrast, is underlain predominantly by sedimentary rocks, so the countryside is softer and more undulating. In most cases these different landscape types are determined by changes in the underlying bedrock which, in turn, are a legacy of Scotland's eventful geological past.

Southern Uplands and the Tweed Valley

The undulating countryside of the Scottish Borders is perhaps less dramatic than the rugged lands to the north, but it has its own particular appeal. The Southern Uplands are built almost entirely of the alternating sequences of sandstones and shales which accumulated on the floor of the Iapetus Ocean separating Scotland from England for many millions of years. The rocks were baked hard when they were buried and heated during this mountain-building process. However, over time, the high peaks were worn down by ice, wind and water, creating the gentle undulations which are now evident.

View of Kirkhope Law, south of Peebles - rolling hills carved in
folded ocean floor sediments which build the Southern Uplands

Midland Valley

The term Midland Valley describes the major geological terrane between the Southern Uplands Fault to the south and the Highland Boundary Fault to the north. The term 'valley', however, is misleading as the topography reflects many different rock types as well as the effects of ice and water erosion and more recent sea-level changes.

The predominant rocks are sandstones and conglomerates with local concentrations of coal from Ayrshire to East Lothian. For the most part, these rocks provide gently undulating topography rising generally to around 100m above sea level. More prominent is the landscape of the igneous rocks. The basaltic lavas form major upland masses, predominant being the Pentlands, Ochils, Sidlaws, Campsies and Kilsyth Hills. The remnants of volcanoes are a singular form in the landscape, for example, the 'laws' of North Berwick, Traprain and Largo, along with the seven hills of Edinburgh. Smoothing and plucking by ice are very pronounced on all of these hills and similar ones, and all show a very distinct east/west orientation. Interestingly, Glasgow is built on a field of drumlins made of till.

The three major river valleys, Clyde, Forth and Tay, have been deepened by the ice and are now infilled with great thicknesses of sediment. Around their shores are fine sequences of terraces left when the sea level fell. The more exposed coasts have rock platforms formed at an earlier period of the Quaternary.

Characteristic features of the Midland Valley in the Stirling area with the volcanic outcrops of the Wallace Monument and Stirling Castle Rock and the flat carselands of the upper Forth with the Ochil Fault between them

47

Eastern Highlands

The landscape of the Eastern Highlands is dominated by the mountain massifs of the East Grampians, predominantly the Cairngorms and the Monadhliaths, sandwiched between the Great Glen Fault and the Highland Boundary Fault. The area comprises generally red granites which have been exposed at the surface since at least the early Tertiary period, surrounded by predominantly Dalradian crystalline rocks. A few significant faults have created lines of weakness which ice and water have exploited, for example, Glen Tilt.

The landscape owes much to weathering during the humid climates of the Tertiary period and the later effects of ice and meltwater. The rolling plateaux with relict tors and the easterly flowing river systems contrast with the steep sides of corries and glacial troughs. The slopes, covered with debris from the ice, have been reworked into many forms since the end of the Ice Age and are still on the move under extreme circumstances such as flash floods and avalanches. The valley basins reflect weathering and erosion over some 50 million years of Earth history. During the last glacial period the valley bottoms were chokcd with glacial debris which has subsequently been reworked into terraces right down to the present river levels.

The Cairngorms and Monadhliath mountains with glacial troughs and rolling plateaux
separated by the Spey Valley with many glacial deposits and modern floodplains

Western Highlands

The Western Highlands are Scotland's premier mountain and loch landscape, formed predominantly of Moine schists. The rocks of the angular peaks and ridges are very resistant to erosion. The mountain topography is rugged as a result of ice action and later periglacial activity.

Steep-sided and very deep valleys penetrate the mountain areas. Formed originally by streams flowing into the newly opening Atlantic, they are short and have very steep gradients. Most have been deepened and straightened by ice action. Some are now filled with sediments deposited during the Ice Age, some filled with fresh water forming numerous lochs, and others filled with sea water where their beds extend well below sea level. Around their fringes are remnants of beaches from periods of higher sea level and in places large accumulations of sand.

On the western seaboard and on the islands of Mull, Rum and Skye, rock types have a more pronounced effect on the landscape. Here the basaltic lavas, best seen on Mull and Skye, give a stepped landscape and the remains of volcanoes, especially the Cuillin of Rum and Skye, form significant mountain groups.

Dramatic scenery characteristic of the Western Highlands with relative relief from mountain top to sea floor of almost 2,000m. Water and ice have been the formative agents of this landscape

Moray Firth and Caithness

Chanonry Point guards the inner Moray Firth. It has developed in post glacial times in response to the movement of sand and gravel along the coastline. Here and elsewhere along this coast are massive accumulations of sands (e.g. at Culbin) and the coast is still extending seawards. The firth itself was excavated during the Ice Age by glaciers moving north-eastwards and later occupied by the sea as water levels rose in response to the melting of the ice. Inland, the bedrock of red sandstones gives a gently undulating landscape subtly moulded by the ice as it scoured the bedrock.

Further to the north the red sandstones give Caithness its predominantly flat appearance with the sentinenl quartizite hills of Scaraben and Morven on its southern edge. This is the land of the blanket bog - thick carpets of sphagnum and many pools which have built up over the last few millennia. High humidity and rainfall along with the poor drainage characteristics of the subsoil and bedrock produce conditions which are ideal for this habitat to develop and thrive.

Blanket bog of the Flow Country

Chanonry Point - the coastline is a recent landscape. Tides, wind and waves have moulded the coastline since the end of the Ice Age

Northwest Highlands

This area of Scotland is known the world over for the grandeur of its scenery. Rugged peaks of Torridonian sandstone, sometimes capped by Cambrian quartzite, rise from an undulating base of Lewisian gneiss, ground down to a characteristic lochan-strewn surface by the passage of ice. The isolated sandstone peaks were at one time part of a continuous cover which buried the gneiss to a depth of a kilometre or more. This is described as an 'exhumed' landscape. Although heavily glaciated, some of the landscape features of the Lewisian surface are those which were present when the Torridonian sediments were deposited some 800 million years ago. Slioch, on the north shore of Loch Maree, illustrates one of the most obvious examples of a landscape which developed during Lewisian times. A 'valley' cut into a bedrock of gneiss was later infilled by Torridonian sediments, so providing the keen observer with a glimpse of an earlier landscape.

Suilven sits on a platform of Lewisian gneiss

Slioch from across Loch Maree - a 'valley' cut in Lewisian gneiss is infilled by Torridonian sandstone

Hebridean Islands

The Outer Hebrides are founded almost entirely on the ancient and hard Lewisian gneisses. The landscape which has developed is, however, quite varied. The high ground of Harris and South Lewis and the spine of hills which runs from North Uist to Barra are rounded and smoothed and have very little debris or soil on their surfaces.

Much of Lewis is low lying, and high humidity, high rainfall and poor drainage have resulted in the formation of extensive areas of blanket peat, similar to those in the Flow Country.

The Hebrides are perhaps best known for the 'machair'; the plain of calcareous shell sand which stretches down the west coast. The rich 'soil' and the particular type of cultivation have resulted in very rich flora and outstanding flowering plants during the summer. This is a cultural rather than a natural landscape. Looking more closely at the landscape, we find an amazing succession of types: the offshore rock reefs, the sandy floor of the sea bed, the small dune ridge now being eroded because of stormier conditions, the machair itself, a substantial number of small lochs (usually freshwater but occasionally brackish water), then an area of blanket peat, and finally the high ground which is interspersed with sea lochs.

The diverse landscape of South Uist showing the classic sequence of rock reefs, sandy beaches, dunes and machair plains, the drowned inland landscape, the peatlands and then the rock ridges

Northern Isles

The geology of the Northern Isles is similar to that of the
Scottish Highlands, and the archipelagoes of Orkney
and Shetland which were extensively glaciated during
the Ice Age. The igneous and metamorphic rocks of
Shetland have a predominantly north/south trend which
gives the landscape a pronounced ridge and valley
topography. The glaciers deepened the pre-existing
valleys, which were later flooded to form the distinctive
sea lochs, known locally as voes, when the ice melted
around 14,000 years ago and the sea level rose,
Weisdale Voe is typical of the coastal scenery on
Shetland. As well as moulding the landscape into gentle
curves, the ice also left a thin mantle of rock debris,
consisting of boulders, stones, sand and clay which
smoothed out irregularities in the bedrock on the lower
slopes of the valleys.

Old Man of Hoy sculpted in
sandstone of Devonian age

Weisdale Voe, Shetland, deepened by glaciers and flooded when the ice melted

Scottish Natural Heritage and the British Geological Survey

Scottish Natural Heritage is a government body. Its aim is to help people enjoy Scotland's natural heritage responsibly, understand it more fully and use it wisely so it can be sustained for future generations.

Scottish Natural Heritage
Great Glen House, Leachkin Road,
Inverness IV3 8NW
t: 01463 725000
e: enquiries@snh.gov.uk

Scottish Natural Heritage
Dualchas Nàdair na h-Alba
All of nature for all of Scotland
Nàdar air fad airson Alba air fad

The British Geological Survey maintains up-to-date knowledge of the geology of the UK and its continental shelf. It carries out surveys and geological research.

The Scottish Office of BGS is sited in Edinburgh. The office runs an advisory and information service, a geological library and a well-stocked geological bookshop.

British Geological Survey
Murchison House
West Mains Road
Edinburgh EH9 3LA
t : 0131 667 1000
f : 0131 668 2683

British
Geological Survey
NATURAL ENVIRONMENT RESEARCH COUNCIL

About the Authors

Alan McKirdy has worked in conservation for over thirty years. He has played a variety of roles during that period; latterly as Head of Information Management at SNH. Alan has edited the Landscape Fashioned by Geology series since its inception and anticipates the completion of this 20 title series shortly. He has written books or book chapters on the geology of Scotland, environmental geology, engineering geology, mineral resource management, geology and landscapes, geo-tourism, geoconservation, the Enlightenment figure, Dr. James Hutton and books for children that introduce younger readers to the rocks, fossils and the landscapes of Scotland.

Roger Crofts CBE was Chief Executive of SNH from its establishment in 1992 until 2002. He trained as a geographer, spent 8 years as a geomorphological researcher and has studied and written about the natural landscape of Scotland. Roger is keen for the public to gain a greater understanding and enjoyment of its history, diversity and dynamism and hopes that this book will help.

Also in the Landscape Fashioned by Geology series...

Arran and the Clyde Islands
David McAdam & Steve Robertson
ISBN 1 85397 287 8
Pbk 24pp £3.00

Ben Nevis and Glencoe
David Stephenson & Kathryn Goodenough
ISBN 1 85397 506 6
Pbk 44pp £4.95

Cairngorms
John Gordon, Rachel Wignall, Ness Brazier,
& Patricia Bruneau
ISBN 1 85397 455 2
Pbk 52pp £4.95

East Lothian and the Borders
David McAdam & Phil Stone
ISBN 1 85397 242 8
Pbk 26pp £3.00

Edinburgh and West Lothian
David McAdam
ISBN 1 85397 327 0
Pbk 44pp £4.95

Fife and Tayside
Mike Browne, Alan McKirdy & David McAdam
ISBN 1 85397 110 3
Pbk 36pp £3.95

Glasgow and Ayrshire
Colin MacFadyen & John Gordon
ISBN 1 85397 451 X
Pbk 52pp £4.95

Glen Roy
Douglas Peacock, John Gordon & Frank May
ISBN 1 85397 360 2
Pbk 36pp £4.95

Loch Lomond to Stirling
Mike Browne & John Mendum
ISBN 1 85397 119 7
Pbk 26pp £2.00

Mull and Iona
David Stephenson
ISBN 1 85397 423 4
Pbk 44pp £4.95

Northeast Scotland
Jon Merritt & Graham Leslie
ISBN 978 1 85397 521 9
Pbk 76pp Price £7.95

Northwest Highlands
John Mendum, Jon Merritt & Alan McKirdy
ISBN 1 85397 139 1
Pbk 52pp £6.95

Orkney and Shetland
Alan McKirdy
ISBN 978 1 85397 602 5
Pbk 68pp £7.95

The Outer Hebrides
Kathryn Goodenough & Jon Merritt
ISBN 1 978185397 507 3
Pbk 44pp £4.95

Rum and the Small Isles
Kathryn Goodenough & Tom Bradwell
ISBN 1 85397 370 2
Pbk 48pp £5.95

Skye
David Stephenson & Jon Merritt
ISBN 1 85397 026 3
Pbk 24pp £3.95

Southwest Scotland
Andrew McMillan & Phil Stone
ISBN 978 1 85397 520 2
Pbk 48pp £4.95

Series Editor: Alan McKirdy (SNH)
Other books soon to be produced in the
series include: Argyll & the Islands and
Moray & Caithness.

To order these and other publications, visit: www.snh.gov.uk/pubs